Richmond, Virginia: Historical Guide for Travelers

American Cities History Guidebook Series

Henry Church

Published by Fiel LLC, 2023.

RICHMOND, VIRGINIA: HISTORICAL GUIDE FOR TRAVELERS

First edition. September 4, 2023.

ISBN: 979-8215189627

Written by Henry Church.

Also by Henry Church

American Cities History Guidebook Series
Charlottesville, Virginia: Historical Guide for Travelers
Williamsburg, Virginia: Historical Guide for Travelers
Richmond, Virginia: Historical Guide for Travelers
Norfolk & Virginia Beach: Historical Guide for Travelers
Winchester, Virginia: Historical Guide for Travelers
Baltimore, Maryland: Historical Guide for Travelers
Dover, Delaware: Historical Guide for Travelers
Arlington, Virginia: Historical Guide for Travelers

Table of Contents

Introduction

Richmond, Virginia, a city with a history as illustrious as the land that surrounds it, has witnessed the creation of heroes, the rise and fall of empires, and the passage of time. Its tale, which is entwined with the American narrative itself, is one of resiliency, ingenuity, hardship, and victory. Richmond is more than just a location on a map; it is a tangible reminder of the history of America, from its early inception to its significance now.

This book seeks to untangle the complex web of Richmond's past by exploring its early years, important turning points in its history, and the people who gave it life. You will be taken on a tour of a certain period or aspect of Richmond's development in each chapter. We'll follow in the steps of the early settlers, experience the revolutionary zeal of the locals, see the difficulties brought on by civil wars and societal changes, and appreciate the technological and cultural apex points that have shaped the city in the twenty-first century.

We'll explore Richmond's architectural wonders, its cultural influences, and the economic factors that have fueled its expansion through the lens of time. We'll get to know the people who made Richmond famous and learn about the social movements that developed or gained momentum there.

Richmond's story, though, is about more than just looking back; it's also about comprehending the present and conceiving of the future. As we examine Richmond's history, we'll also shed light on the contemporary issues and innovations the city is facing, providing readers an idea of where Richmond might be going in the future.

This book provides a thorough and interesting tour of Richmond's history, whether you're a local curious about your town, a student interested in its past, or a visitor eager to learn more about this American treasure. In order to learn more about the events and legacies that have shaped Richmond, Virginia into the metropolis it is today, let's set off on this historical journey.

Chapter 1: Native Tribes of Richmond

The region was a patchwork of varied cultures, traditions, and communities that had flourished for centuries before the colonists' ships graced the shores of Virginia or the skyline of contemporary Richmond rose against the horizon. Native tribes that originally lived in the area around Richmond had a significant impact on its history and laid the groundwork for its future.

The Powhatan Confederacy comes to mind when one considers native tribes in Richmond and the areas around it. Chief Powhatan, the paramount chief of this mighty confederation of Algonquian-speaking tribes, presided over a wide territory that included much of Virginia's Tidewater region. The Powhatan people were semi-sedentary, engaged in a combination of agriculture, hunting, and fishing, and lived in villages.

The Powhatan people found the confluence of the James River and its tributaries to be a fertile and bountiful region, and they built many towns along these waters. They peppered the countryside with their longhouse-and-palisade-enclosed villages.

The Powhatan Confederacy's tribal members shared similar cultural customs and worldviews. The "Three Sisters" (corn, beans, and squash) were a major source of food for them. This trio of crops, which symbolized the interdependence of life, were entwined not just in their farming techniques but also in their spiritual beliefs.

Their communities placed a high value on ceremonies and rituals. The Okeus was the main deity attributed to both good and bad luck in the Powhatan hierarchy of spirits and gods. Rituals, dances, and feasts were frequently used to pay homage to these deities, assure abundant harvests, and mark significant life occasions.

The local tribes saw significant changes as a result of the introduction of English settlers in the early 17th century. The Powhatan people and the newcomers initially interacted out of curiosity and hesitant trade. Conflicts, however, were unavoidable as the English colonies flourished and their demand for land increased.

One of the most well-known tales from this time is about Pocahontas, the daughter of Chief Powhatan, and her contacts with the Jamestown colony. Her story, despite being frequently romanticized, is a witness to the complexity of the relationships between the indigenous tribes and the Europeans.

The Powhatan Confederacy's dominance gradually started to decline due to the influx of diseases brought by the settlers, land encroachment, and frequent battles. its power had greatly decreased by the late 17th century, and many of its tribes had been dispersed or assimilated.

But the history of Richmond continues to be profoundly influenced by the legacy of the Powhatan and other indigenous groups. The names given by the tribes are still used for landmarks, rivers, and place names. Their attitude is a tribute to the fortitude and tenacity of the people who called Richmond home long before it was known by that name, and their influence can be seen in the city's cultural tapestry.

In the chapters that follow, we'll look at how the foundation these tribes built allowed Richmond to develop from a colonial outpost to a significant historical metropolis. But as we delve more into Richmond's past, let us not disregard its original residents, the native tribes whose tales, hardships, and legacies continue to shape the city.

Chapter 2: Early Settlers and Their Stories

The wide and varied New World lured European explorers and immigrants as the 17th century ushered in, promising enormous riches, fertile fields, and a new beginning. With its advantageous location along the James River, the area around Richmond quickly became a focal focus for these early inhabitants. Their stories of tenacity, aspiration, and struggle with the local tribes create an engrossing chapter in Richmond's history.

The first permanent English settlement in the New World was established at Jamestown in 1607. Even though Jamestown was located downstream of the present-day city of Richmond, it served as a catalyst for future exploration and settlement up the James River. The river's navigability, fertile territory ideal for growing tobacco, and potential trade opportunities with local tribes all attracted settlers.

John Rolfe: John Rolfe was a notable early immigrant from England who is most recognized for establishing tobacco farming as a lucrative cash crop. Rolfe's union with Pocahontas, the daughter of the Powhatan chief, was his other noteworthy historical accomplishment. Although fleeting, their union symbolized a transient truce between the settlers and the Powhatan Confederacy.

Thomas Stegg: Thomas Stegg is a different settler whose name is inscribed in the history of Richmond. He founded a trading post higher up the James River in the early 1640s, making it one of the first English colonies in the Richmond region.

William Byrd II: Richmond's importance increased as the 17th century gave way to the 18th, and so did its list of noteworthy settlers. William Byrd II had a crucial role in the founding of Richmond as a city. He was given the responsibility of surveying the line separating Virginia and

North Carolina when he realized the potential of the area around the James River Falls. Byrd not only supported Richmond's founding but also contributed to its layout.

As they attempted to establish a living in this foreign area, the early settlers faced many difficulties. Malaria was among the health issues brought on by the marshy environment along the James River. The tribes who lived there were subject to unpredictable relations that alternated between peaceful trade and brutal conflict.

However, the assurance of prosperity kept them grounded. Virginia's economic foundation was tobacco farming, which was made possible by the abundant soil. With the expansion of plantations, settlements developed into towns with a sad and increasing reliance on labor provided by African slaves.

Richmond was first established in 1737 as a result of the persistent efforts of settlers like William Byrd II. Due to the stunning similarity between the James River perspective and that of the River Thames, Byrd is said to have named the city Richmond upon Thames after Richmond upon Thames in England. Richmond was destined for expansion from the beginning. Due to its riverfront location, it was a natural center for trade and would soon play a significant role in the development of American history.

The narratives of the early settlers are ones of optimism, adversity, ambition, and resiliency. These early settlers established the groundwork for a city that would experience revolutions, civil wars, and societal changes, whether they were pursuing wealth, escaping persecution, or looking for a fresh start. Understanding and appreciating these early years is crucial as we proceed through Richmond's history since they paved the way for everything that came after. Even now, Richmond's identity is still rooted in the pioneering spirit of the frontier, which was characterized by persistence and vision.

Chapter 3: Richmond in the Colonial Era

The United States underwent a transformation throughout the colonial era. This period was marked by growth, economic development, and a growing understanding of Richmond's strategic importance within the greater colonial environment for the city situated along the James River.

Because of its unique location next to the James River Falls, Richmond served as a hub for trade. The falls served as a natural place for the movement of commodities even if they served as a navigational barrier for ships. The region's gold, tobacco, was bundled into hogsheads and transported to Richmond's ports where it was transshipped to England and other European markets.

With the popularity of this sector came people and a wide range of abilities. In Richmond, blacksmiths, coopers, and merchants opened their doors to serve the needs of both the local populace and traveling traders.

The colonial society was woven from several threads. Plantation owners and wealthy businessmen at the top possessed influence and power in the economy. They paid homage to the culture and traditions from across the Atlantic with luxurious residences and lifestyles that resembled those of the English.

However, the enslaved were the ones driving the economy, especially the lucrative tobacco sector. During this time, the bitter effects of slavery were firmly ingrained in Richmond's social and economic structure. While the affluent few profited, the African populace that was enslaved went through hardships and had their freedoms and rights violated.

The native tribes, who were formerly the dominant forces in the area, noticed a decline in their dominance. Their population and authority drastically decreased as a result of settlers' encroachment on their territory and the terrible effects of the diseases they carried.

In the colonial period, religion was crucial. The colony's official religion was the Anglican Church. Churches frequently acted as communal hubs and spaces for civic gatherings in addition to being places of worship.

Although appreciated, education was not yet as institutionalized as it would be in the future. Wealthy families frequently sent their kids to England for school or hired private tutors. Others received less formal schooling that concentrated on the fundamentals of literacy and math.

Richmond's expansion and wealth by the middle of the 18th century were at conflict with the colonial connection with England in an increasing amount of ways. Due to its commercial linkages and growing civic awareness, the city developed a strong pro-revolutionary spirit.

A significant occasion was the Richmond-based Virginia Convention of 1775. It symbolized Virginia's choice to send soldiers to the Continental Army. One of Virginia's most notable individuals, Patrick Henry, expressed the rising sense of revolt in his famous "Give me liberty, or give me death!" speech at Richmond's St. John's Church.

Colonial times paved the way for Richmond's significant place in American history. Richmond was not only a witness to but also an active player in the events that would result in the formation of a nation, from its growth as a trading hub to its place in the revolutionary fever. The effect of these colonial underpinnings on Richmond's destiny becomes clear as we dive into the next chapters, highlighting the city's importance in the larger fabric of American history.

Chapter 4: Important Landmarks and their History

Richmond's rich past is imprinted in its brick, mortar, and environment in addition to in records and stories. The city is home to several famous landmarks, each of which has a tale to tell about how it has stood as a quiet witness to the tides of time. The origins and historical significance of some of Richmond's most recognizable landmarks will be explored in this chapter.

St. John's Church

Origin: St. John's Church was built in 1741 and is the oldest wooden church in Virginia that is still in use today.

Significance: In addition to having stunning architecture, this cathedral served as the venue for the Second Virginia Convention in 1775, which is where Patrick Henry gave his well-known "Give me liberty or give me death" speech, igniting the American Revolution.

The State House of Virginia

Origin: The Virginia State Capitol, designed by Thomas Jefferson and finished in 1788, is home to the oldest elected legislative body in the New World.

Meaning: It has served as a hub for legislative initiatives and crucial political choices that have affected both Virginia and the rest of the country over the years.

Monument Avenue

Grandiose statues honoring Confederate leaders can be found on Monument Avenue in Richmond, Virginia. The late 19th and early 20th centuries saw the construction of these sculptures, which included notable individuals including Robert E. Lee, J.E.B. Stuart, Jefferson Davis, Stonewall Jackson, and Matthew Fontaine Maury. Over time, they evolved into a contentious representation of racism, white supremacy, and historical oppression for many, in addition to serving as a tribute to the South's commemoration of the Civil War.

These sculptures began to be a source of controversy when American society underwent major change, particularly in the late 20th and early 21st centuries. These monuments received fresh attention as a result of the campaign against structural racism and police brutality, which culminated in activities like the Black Lives Matter demonstrations. They were criticized for romanticizing individuals who upheld slavery and continued racial injustice, according to critics, and for representing an outmoded and damaging narrative.

The fate of the statues was a hot topic of discussion throughout the 2010s and 2020s. Some sculptures were destroyed or overturned by activists during protests, public uproar, and calls for their removal. Conflicts between those who wanted the sculptures to stay and those who wanted them taken down occasionally caused tensions to rise.

The official position on these statues has likewise changed. Recognizing the suffering and divide they represented, some local governments and organizations started legal removal or relocation procedures. In June 2020, protesters toppled the Jefferson Davis statue in Richmond. Later, in September 2021, the Robert E. Lee statue was demolished pursuant to a formal order. Similar things happened to other statues on Monument Avenue, either being torn down forcibly by protesters or being taken down by the authorities.

For many, the removal or demolition of these statues served as a sign of rejection of historical accounts that exalted racial tyranny. Some people lamented the loss of what they saw as a fundamental component of

Southern legacy, while others rejoiced in it as a step toward a more thorough and accurate understanding of American history.

The area where the monuments formerly stood has been transformed into a forum for discourse, memorial, and public expression. The ideal way to utilize these areas to promote harmony, education, and a deeper comprehension of the nation's complicated past is still being discussed.

Tredegar Iron Works

The Confederacy's main supplier for cannons, ammunition, and other warfare supplies, this complex was established in 1837.

Significance: The American Civil War Museum is now located there, showcasing the rich industrial and military heritage of Richmond.

Maymont

Origin: Maymont, a 100-acre Victorian house that was finished in 1893, is a prime example of the splendor of Richmond's upper class during the Gilded Age.

Significance: The estate is significant because it exemplifies the socioeconomic dynamics of Richmond in the late 19th century through its spectacular buildings, gardens, and wildlife.

Belle Isle

Origin: Originally a fishing spot for local tribes, this island in the James River underwent transformation throughout the years, working as a fishery, an iron mill, and a prison camp during the Civil War.

Meaning: Belle Isle, now a well-liked park, has a complex past that sheds light on Richmond's multifaceted development.

The Museum of Edgar Allan Poe

Origin: This museum honors the life and work of the renowned American author who grew up in Richmond and is housed in the oldest standing structure in the city, which dates back to the 1730s.

Significance: Beyond its connection to Poe, the structure is significant as a remnant of colonial architecture and early Richmond life.

Historic District of Broad Street

Origin: Broad Street, a significant commercial avenue since the 18th century, witnessed the growth of the city as a whole.

Significance: Today, it represents Richmond's fusion of old and new with its mix of historic structures and contemporary businesses.

Chapter 5: Richmond during the American Revolution

Richmond's strategic and symbolic significance increased dramatically as hostilities between the British colonies in the Americas and Great Britain reached a breaking point. We shall look into Richmond's crucial role during the tumultuous years of the American Revolution in this chapter.

Richmond had established itself as a hub for revolutionary speech long before the first bullets were fired at Lexington and Concord. Richmond's salons, bars, and churches were hopping with discussions of freedom, representation, and self-determination.

Important individuals, such as Patrick Henry and Richard Henry Lee, frequently occupied the middle of Richmond's public squares to promote independence and mobilize the local population against what they saw to be British tyranny.

Virginia served as the Revolution's hub. A sign of Richmond's growing importance is the fact that it became Virginia's capital in 1780. However, this action also turned it become a top target for British operations. A devastating incident that exposed the frailties and expenses of the revolutionary cause occurred just a year later, in 1781, when British forces under the command of the traitor Benedict Arnold burned down much of the city.

Although important pitched battles were not fought in Richmond as they were in other colonies, it was still essential to the supply and logistics of the revolutionary troops. The city served as a vital hub for the revolutionary leadership's communication, accommodation of troops, and storage of weapons.

Local militias constructed defensive lines all around Richmond as British reconnaissance units engaged in skirmishes and a cat-and-mouse game with them.

Richmond's burgeoning economic activities were hampered by the war. British blockades caused the once-active docks to become less active, requiring the city to invent and adapt. While some business owners were in financial trouble, others turned to the war industry and provided the Continental Army with supplies and equipment.

The revolutionary spirit also heightened discussions about slavery, laying the groundwork for upcoming conflicts. The Revolution's emphasis on liberty and equality did not go unnoticed by the population of slaves, even if the institution mostly survived, paving the way for later liberation campaigns.

Richmond was crucial to the Revolution because of its closeness to Yorktown. Richmond acted as a supply and communication connection for the Franco-American soldiers as the pivotal Siege of Yorktown began in 1781. As soon as word of Lord Cornwallis's capitulation reached Richmond, street parties broke out.

Chapter 6: Local Heroes and Events of Note

The histories of Richmond's heroes—sung and unsung—and the crucial occasions they took part in are intertwined with the legacy of the city during the American Revolution. These individuals and events become enduring symbols in Richmond's collective memory, capturing the essence and character of the city.

Patrick Henry: The Revolution's Voice

Patrick Henry was a native of Hanover County, which is a suburb of Richmond, and his passionate speeches came to represent the spirit of the American Revolution. Given in St. John's Church in Richmond, his "Give me liberty, or give me death!" speech inspired many to support the cause of revolution and established Richmond as a hotbed of resistance.

A Call for Independence from Richard Henry Lee

Lee, a second Virginian, played a key role in the Continental Congress's drive for independence. The Declaration of Independence was written and adopted as a direct result of his decision in June 1776. Lee's influences and roots were deeply rooted in Virginia, despite the fact that most of his work was produced in Philadelphia.

Fire in 1781

The raid that was led by the traitor Benedict Arnold left a permanent mark on Richmond. Although there was substantial material destruction, there was also severe psychological harm. The burning of Richmond became a symbol of the city's tenacity and will as well as a scar from the conflict.

Elizabeth Van Lew: Richmond's Spy

Elizabeth Van Lew's revolutionary ancestry helped to shape her commitment to the Union, even though her most significant contributions to the war came later. Elizabeth was raised with a strong sense of patriotism by her father, John Van Lew, who actively promoted the revolutionary cause.

Gabriel's Rebellion of 1800

Although this event took place after the Revolution, the rhetoric of liberty and equality from that time period served as its seeds. The Richmond slaveholding class was the target of a massive uprising that Gabriel, an enslaved blacksmith, planned. Despite being put down, the revolt highlighted the fundamental inconsistencies of a society that fought for freedom but denied it to many of its people.

The Camp Charlotte Treaty (1774)

There was a major event that affected the area before the Revolution took center stage. Lord Dunmore's War hostilities were put an end by the treaty that was reached between the Colony of Virginia and the Shawnee and Mingo Native American tribes. Vast new areas were made accessible to Virginian settlers, but it further disenfranchised the native population.

Midnight Ride by Jack Jouett (1781)

Jack Jouett, known as "the Paul Revere of the South," is renowned for his legendary 40-mile ride through the Virginia countryside to alert Thomas Jefferson and the Virginia legislature to an oncoming British attack. The majority of the lawmakers managed to avoid captivity thanks to Jouett, maintaining the independence of Virginia's revolutionary government.

Chapter 7: Post-Revolution Changes and Development

The American Revolution represented a critical turning point for Richmond as well as the young United States. Richmond witnessed significant changes when the smoke cleared and the new country made its first tentative moves, paving the way for its rise to prominence as a key American metropolis.

As soon as the battle was finished, Richmond started to develop into a hub of government and trade. Virginia's capital was moved from Williamsburg to Richmond in 1780, replacing the colonial capital. Along with governmental activity, this change also brought a surge of professionals, business owners, and settlers.

Following the Revolution, Richmond's advantageous location on the James River became even more apparent. Trade became dependent on the river, and plans were made to make it more navigable and build canals. Although it wasn't really built until much later in the 19th century, the James River and Kanawha Canal was initially planned to ease trade routes to the American West.

After the war, Richmond's cultural scene flourished. Theaters, libraries, and salons started to appear as institutions. Established in the late 18th century, the Richmond Theatre quickly rose to prominence as a hub for entertainment and creative expression.

Richmond started to diversify its economic basis even while tobacco remained a big economic engine. Utilizing the city's advantageous position and expanding infrastructure, mills, workshops, and small manufacturing businesses arose.

The Revolution's ideas persisted, igniting debates on social issues, most notably slavery. Even while the institution was still strong, there was growing disquiet, especially among the educated upper class of the city. Manumissions rose, and a free Black community started to quietly but surely expand.

With the new republic's emphasis on education, attempts were made to set up educational institutions. The establishment of Richmond Academy in the 1790s marked the start of the city's organized educational system.

As with every time of growth, difficulties appeared. Urban planning, public safety, and government were among the problems the new state capital had to address. A city charter was enacted in 1782, establishing municipal structures and granting Richmond more power over its administration.

As international trade restarted, activity on Richmond's docks increased. Additionally, once the war came to a conclusion, European officials, traders, and tourists arrived in the city, bringing with them global influences and connections.

Chapter 8: Industry and Infrastructure Growth

Richmond's status as the state capital of Virginia and its fortunate location on the James River at the beginning of the 19th century made it a prime location for industrial growth and expansion. The post-Revolutionary period's sowings started to bear fruit, and the city witnessed a physical and economic makeover.

The early industrial endeavors of Richmond were inextricably linked to its agricultural foundations. Virginia's economy, which is based largely on tobacco, took center stage. As tobacco warehouses and processing plants proliferated, Richmond became a major player in the industry. Cotton mills started to arise at the same time, mirroring a larger trend in the American South. Additionally thriving was the flour milling sector, with Richmond's mills being known for their superior output.

However, the development and expansion of the iron industry represented the real paradigm shift. Foundries and manufacturing businesses sprang developed, taking use of the abundant iron reserves in the area. These factories increased Richmond's economic impact by producing goods for both export and local use.

This industrial boom was illustrated by the establishment of the Tredegar Iron Works in the early 1830s. It quickly rose to prominence as one of the country's most productive ironworks, producing everything from locomotives to artillery. It had solidified its position as a cornerstone of the Southern industrial landscape by the eve of the Civil War.

Infrastructure was improved and expanded in tandem with industrial growth. The James River's potential as a route for transit was recognized, and efforts to improve its navigability increased. The James River and Kanawha Canal, in particular, sought to offer a direct water connection from Richmond to the western territories. Although the canal was never able to reach its original location, it was crucial in promoting trade and transit inside Virginia.

The new age's technological marvel, railroads, also started to leave its mark on Richmond. Established in the 1830s, the Richmond, Fredericksburg & Potomac Railroad and the Virginia Central Railroad gave Richmond access to vital markets and resources. In the years to come, particularly during the American Civil War, this rail infrastructure would prove to be important.

These changes did not come without difficulties. The expansion of industry had societal effects. The sometimes unfavorable working conditions in the mills and foundries prompted strikes and calls for better circumstances from the workforce. The discussion over slavery grew more heated as industry expanded. While some argued that enslaved labor was essential to the Southern economic paradigm, others supported a shift to a system that was more wage-based.

The growing infrastructure presented further difficulties. Large infrastructure projects like railroads and canals needed a lot of money to be financed, which prompted complex collaborations between the state government and private industry. Making decisions about routes and priorities frequently become acrimonious, reflecting a larger conflict between regional demands and state-wide objectives.

Despite these obstacles, Richmond had evolved by the middle of the 19th century from a predominantly agricultural town to a booming industrial city. The two pillars of infrastructure and industry built a solid base, preparing Richmond for the turbulent but momentous events of the ensuing decades.

Chapter 9: Richmond During the Civil War

Richmond was forced into the center of the impending conflict as the nation's divisions widened in the 19th century. When the Confederate States of America were established in 1861, Richmond was chosen as the nation's capital, a choice that would determine the course of the following four years for the city.

Richmond was picked with purpose. The Tredegar Iron Works in particular, part of its industrial backbone, promised to provide the Confederacy with crucial war supplies. The city's location provided a fortified position and was close enough to Washington, D.C., the capitol of the Union, to maintain pressure on the North. Richmond, though, became a top target for Union soldiers as a result of their close proximity.

The seriousness of the war was evident in Richmond right away. The city turned into a hub of Confederate government activity, including legislative meetings and military planning conferences. As President Jefferson Davis and his government established themselves, the city became the Confederacy's political hub.

The human cost of the war was evident on the streets of Richmond. The city's hospitals were built to accommodate the influx of wounded soldiers from adjacent battlefields. Over 75,000 patients were treated at the Chimborazo Hospital, one of the biggest military hospitals during the Civil War.

People in the city were heavily involved in the war effort. Women started working as nurses, military uniform seamstresses, and aid society administrators. Local enterprises were adjusted to produce everything from shoes to ammunition for the Confederate armies throughout the conflict.

However, there were difficulties in daily living in the Confederate capital. As the battle continued on, shortages were experienced often. Rationing of food, clothing, and other needs made life more difficult, and the falling value of the Confederate currency made matters worse.

From 1864 to 1865, the Siege of Petersburg was a turning moment for Richmond. Both resources and morale were depleted by the protracted engagement. Confederate officials, including President Davis, departed Richmond in April 1865 after realizing the city was about to fall. Parts of the city were destroyed by multiple fires as they fled, either intentionally or unintentionally caused as a scorched-earth strategy.

General Godfrey Weitzel was in charge of the Union forces who entered Richmond on April 3, 1865. A moving image of the destruction caused by the Civil War was the burning city. Residents of Richmond and Union soldiers collaborated to put out the fires and stop more harm.

Richmond was scarred and in ruins after the end of the battle. The people had endured great suffering, and its once-vibrant industrial districts had suffered severe damage. But when the haze cleared, Richmond's tenacious character became apparent. As it dealt with its post-war legacy and looked to the future, the city would set off on a voyage of reconstruction, introspection, and reinterpretation in the years to come.

Chapter 10: Reconstruction and its Impact

Following the Civil War, there were significant political, economic, and social changes throughout the Reconstruction era. As Richmond struggled to adjust to its new reality, the age presented both opportunities and challenges. Richmond was formerly the proud capital of the Confederacy.

The Confederate government and its institutions disintegrated after the war, leaving a void. The goal of the federal government was to bring the former Confederate states back into the Union, and because of Richmond's importance, this process was constantly monitored.

Richmond had an enormous challenge ahead of it economically. The war had severely damaged or destroyed most of its infrastructure. Industries had to be repurposed or completely rebuilt, especially those that had supplied the Confederate war machine. A sharecropping and tenant farming system took the place of the South's slave-based economy. While this was supposed to free African Americans from slavery, the new system frequently kept farmers of all races in a loop of debt and dependency.

Richmond and the rest of the South experienced significant political shift. Military governors were chosen in the early stages of reconstruction to manage the area. Political activism increased dramatically in the city, especially among the newly emancipated African Americans. They campaigned, organized, and participated in elections, which allowed African Americans to be elected to positions they would have never imagined a decade before.

The city was changing socially. The goals of freedmen included reuniting families that had been split up by slavery, starting schools, and establishing new social positions. This was made possible by the Freedmen's Bureau's assistance in legal issues, educational opportunities, and employment agreements.

But opposition to these developments persisted. Many white Richmonders rejected the new order because they were confused by the quick changes and status loss. There were groups like the Ku Klux Klan that used violence and intimidation to halt the advancement of African Americans and reinstate white dominance.

Richmond turned became a flashpoint for these conflicts. It served as a focal point for both African American aspirations and white Southern hatred due to its status as a former Confederate capital. Landmarks like the Virginia State Capitol became the scene of both violent clashes and nonviolent protests.

During this time, education had a transforming impact. Whites and African Americans agreed that it had a significant influence on the New South. The first public schools for black children started operating in Richmond around this time, despite opposition. Several educational institutions that would later develop into well-known universities were created at the same time.

By the time Reconstruction came to a conclusion in 1877, Richmond had undergone a transformation. A new city was arising from the wreckage of conflict and the upheaval of societal transformation. Richmond was changing, despite the deep-seated effects of slavery, segregation, and war scars. Its experience with Reconstruction had prepared it for the struggles and victories of the following 20th century.

Chapter 11: Richmond in the Gilded Age

The Gilded Age, which took place in America between the 1870s and the early 1900s, was a time of significant change and contrast. It was a time of regeneration, creativity, and stark contrasts for Richmond, a city still recuperating from the turmoil of the Civil War and the difficulties of Reconstruction.

Richmond's economy has been reviving. The city experienced a boom in sectors ranging from tobacco to textiles because to its advantageous location and plenty of natural resources. The construction of railroads like the Richmond and Danville Railroad made trading easier and turned Richmond into a thriving commercial center. Businesses like the Virginia-Carolina Chemical Corporation and the American Tobacco Company got their start during this time, and they quickly turned Richmond into a major economic hub in the South.

But the distribution of riches wasn't fair. The term "Gilded Age," popularized by Mark Twain, alludes to the period's sparkling exterior, which hid more significant socioeconomic problems. While businessmen and industrialists prospered, many Richmond residents, particularly the working class, endured harsh circumstances and low earnings. Workers frequently participated in labor protests and strikes in order to get higher wages and safer working conditions.

During this time, Richmond's urban environment started to alter. The increasing riches was reflected in the construction of opulent houses, theaters, and other buildings. Monument Avenue was created and expanded, becoming a representation of Southern pride and a reminder of its tumultuous past with its massive statues honoring Confederate leaders.

Richmond experienced a cultural boom. The patronage of the arts and literature increased along with rising wealth. In the city, libraries, museums, and other cultural organizations were founded. Richmond's status as a hub of Southern culture grew as writers, singers, and artists found both an audience and inspiration there.

However, there was still disagreement regarding race relations. African Americans' gains during Reconstruction were steadily reversed throughout the Gilded Age. Jim Crow laws were put into place, which imposed racial segregation and treated African Americans as second-class citizens. The racial divide grew as a result of these laws and societal prejudices, which restricted opportunities for Black Richmond residents.

Politics added even another level of complexity. The Democratic Party regained power in Virginia by promoting the "Lost Cause" narrative, which idealized the South's contribution to the Civil War and minimized the impact of slavery. For Richmond, this had far-reaching effects that affected everything from educational systems to urban development.

By the end of the Gilded Age, Richmond had undergone yet another transformation. It served as a symbol of the splendor and contrasts of the time. Despite being a city of industry and creativity, it nevertheless coexisted with the problems of the past and the present.

Chapter 12: The Rise of Technology and its Effects

At the dawn of the 20th century, an age of unrivaled technological development began. This resulted in significant adjustments to Richmond's way of life, the economy, and even the cityscape itself.

The industrial foundation of Richmond quickly embraced these modifications. Already a vital component of the city's economy, factories started incorporating modern equipment to increase productivity. For instance, the textile mills included mechanized looms that could create cloth at a rate that was unthinkable just a few decades ago.

Changes in transportation were revolutionary. The advent of the automobile altered how people moved across the city. Initially, cars were a luxury that only a select few could buy, but by the 1910s and 1920s, the middle class could more easily purchase them. Because citizens could dwell further away from the city center and still travel effectively, this enhanced mobility enabled the city to grow outside of its original boundaries. The hum and honk of motor vehicles had replaced the earlier dominance of horse-drawn carriages, streetcars, and pedestrians on the city's streets.

Richmond started to glow with electricity in ways that were previously only imagined. A new era for the city began with the founding of the Virginia Electric & Power Company. Electric lighting brightened the streets, electrified dwellings, and revolutionized daily tasks with electric appliances. This altered not only the daily rhythm but also the length of the productive day, changing social customs and conventions.

Richmond is now more connected than ever because to the development of telecommunications technologies, especially the telephone. The pace of business transactions increased, and distances between locations appeared to close. Through distance, families and friends could still stay in touch, building the social fabric.

These improvements did not come without difficulties, either. Concerns about job losses were raised as industries became more mechanized, particularly among the working class. Labor movements and unions, which had traditionally focused primarily on salaries and working conditions, now had to deal with the effects of automation.

Environmental issues also started to emerge. Pollution rose as the number of cars and enterprises expanded. The city's air was polluted by manufacturers' smoke and automobile emissions, which sparked early conversations about environmental sustainability and health.

Technology has both unified and divided society. While innovations like the radio brought people together through shared information and experiences, they also brought discrepancies to light. Residents of Richmond did not all have equal access to these modern marvels. The disparity, which frequently followed racial and economic lines, served as a sharp reminder that development wasn't always accompanied by equally beneficial outcomes.

The development of technology at the turn of the 20th century was a significant turning point in Richmond's history. It changed how the city interacted with the outside world, reorganized its economic and social systems, and prepared the city for the opportunities and problems of the modern period.

Chapter 13: Richmond during WWI and WWII

Cities within those nations and their nation-states are not exempt from the way that war alters the course of history. The history of Richmond during the World Wars is one of tenacity, adaptation, and change.

Richmond was swept up in the fervor of preparedness as World War I grew closer. Despite the United States' late 1917 entry into the conflict, the city's industrial capabilities changed to serve the war effort. Formerly producing civilian items, these factories were now producing military hardware. With its advantageous location and well-established industrial foundation, Richmond emerged as a major player in this industry as the demand for products like textiles, metals, and tobacco skyrocketed.

However, the impact of WWI on Richmond's society went far beyond just economic change. Numerous young men from the city joined the military or were drafted, leaving behind their families and careers. For the first time, a large number of women filled the positions left vacant by the males in many businesses. This not only increased employment but also signaled the beginning of a gradual change in attitudes on women's roles in society.

Richmond's post-World War I situation was complicated. A surge of wealth arrived during the Roaring Twenties, but the city was severely affected by the Great Depression's ensuing economic slump. The industrial base, which had expanded dramatically during the war, now faced formidable obstacles.

But as the city struggled economically, World War II, another major worldwide conflict, was about to break out. Richmond's industries responded to the call once more. The city's manufacturers shifted to producing items for the war, including uniforms and ammunition.

Further involving the city in the war effort was the Richmond Naval Air Station, which functioned as a focal point for naval operations during the conflict.

During WWII, Richmond's social structure also suffered significant damage. Having been conscripted or enlisted in large numbers, men's traditionally male-dominated roles were once again filled by women. But this time, the adjustment was more significant. The experiences of World War II strengthened the notion that women could perform any job, establishing the foundation for subsequent initiatives for gender equality.

A crucial part was also performed by Richmond's African American community. Many Black Richmonders contributed considerably to the war effort on the home front and on the battlefield, despite still having to deal with Jim Crow's discriminatory laws. This contribution stoked the flames of the fight for equality and civil rights in the years that followed.

Richmond has seen yet another significant alteration by the end of World War II. The wars had hastened the economic development of the city, altered its social mores, and prepared the way for the civil rights movements that would come to define the middle of the 20th century. Richmond emerged from the furnace of these two wars with a fresh sense of identity and purpose, prepared to take on the challenges of the post-war world.

Chapter 14: Military Bases and Economics During WWII

During the turbulent years of World War II, Richmond saw significant economic, social, and political change. Richmond became a key component of America's war effort as a result of the collaboration between the city's economic infrastructure and military facilities.

The Richmond Naval Air Station was at the fore of this transition. It was established in the early 20th century, but WWII gave it utmost significance. It served as a crucial location for naval operations and logistics due to its closeness to the coast. Here, aircraft flew anti-submarine patrols that were essential in the Atlantic campaign against German U-boats. The site additionally operated as a Navy pilot training facility, assuring a consistent influx of newly qualified troops to support the war in Europe and the Pacific.

These military sites have significant economic effects. The bases directly employed thousands of laborers and military. Local businesses benefited from the increase in staff; more people visited restaurants, shops, and entertainment places. The demand for houses near military bases surged, which contributed to expansion in the real estate market.

However, the economic effects extended beyond the military stations' immediate area. The factories in Richmond, which were already crucial to the city's economy, underwent changes during the war. In order to satisfy the demands of the war, industries changed their production processes. Formerly producing just civilian goods, factories now create everything from military outfits to munitions. Federal contracts flooded in as a result of this manufacturing rerouting, giving Richmond's economy a fresh boost.

The city as a whole suffered the effects of this industrial development. People from rural areas and other regions of the state were attracted by the exponential growth in employment prospects. A positive cycle of growth and development was created as a result of the fast urbanization.

This economic boom wasn't without problems, though. Rapid industrialization brought resource allocation problems, labor disputes, and worries about the viability of the post-World War II economy. The city had the difficult problem of making sure that its expansion was manageable and that it could easily transition into a post-war economy.

The employment of women and African Americans was a key component of this time period. Both groups saw fresh prospects in industrial settings and military bases. The wider social movements that would emerge after the war, which would question ingrained social conventions, were forerunners to this economic empowerment.

In essence, Richmond underwent significant changes as a result of World War II's military installations and economic reorientation that went well beyond the conflict itself. The city's struggles at this time, juggling military requirements with economic expansion and social transformation, laid the groundwork for its development in the second half of the 20th century.

Chapter 15: Richmond in the Civil Rights Era

During the Civil Rights Era, Richmond, Virginia, a city with strong Confederate heritage, found itself in a pivotal situation. During this turbulent yet revolutionary time, Richmond's past and present came together as America wrestled with issues of racial justice and equality.

The historical setting of Richmond made the campaign for equality a difficult one. The capital of the Confederacy, Richmond was not just any other southern city. Its streets and structures served as a living memorial to a history that long promoted racial segregation and prejudice. In Richmond, the winds of change encountered resistance and resiliency as they began to blow across America in the 1950s and 1960s.

Virginia's "massive resistance" program was at the fore of this struggle. Virginia's political leaders firmly disagreed with the 1954 Supreme Court decision Brown v. Board of Education, which determined racial segregation in public schools to be unconstitutional. Instead of integrating, schools in Richmond were occasionally closed to avoid it. This approach not only slowed down racial integration in the city but also widened ethnic gaps.

The voices calling for change, however, were just as powerful as the forces of resistance. A ray of optimism and tenacity shone from Richmond's African American community. Local churches were turned into gathering places for civil rights discussions, planning, and mobilization. Leading personalities like Gillfield Baptist Church's Rev. Wyatt Tee Walker came from the clergy, uniting the movement in Richmond with luminaries like Dr. Martin Luther King Jr.

Additionally, students were crucial. Students from Virginia Union University staged their own sit-ins at department store lunch counters all throughout Richmond after being inspired by the sit-ins in Greensboro, North Carolina. These nonviolent demonstrations drew opposition but also major media coverage, raising awareness of the civil rights movement in Richmond.

The 1960s were especially important. Demonstrations, marches, and protests became commonplace. The Richmond Crusade for Voters was established in 1956 with the goal of changing the political climate of the city and putting an end to segregationist and discriminatory practices. They worked relentlessly to register Black voters.

However, there were failures and tragedies throughout this time period as well. Racial tensions frequently descended into violence, with clashes between supporters of the peaceful protestors and those who opposed them in the streets. While tragic, these occurrences only served to bolster Richmond's African American community's resolve.

Real changes started to take shape during the late 1960s and early 1970s. Schools were gradually integrated, but there were difficulties. Discriminatory practices in workplaces, public spaces, and housing were being eliminated more and more, and laws were being updated to reflect this renewed commitment to equality.

The Civil Rights Era journey of Richmond is evidence of the fortitude and tenacity of its people. With its complex past, the city had a difficult road to racial equality. In spite of this, Richmond emerged from this age indelibly changed and moved in the direction of a more inclusive future because to the unwavering spirit of its African American community and supporters.

Chapter 16: Other Notable Social Movements in Richmond

While the Civil Rights Movement had a significant impact on Richmond, other revolutionary social groups that emerged throughout the 20th century also had a significant impact. The city has served as a canvas on which diverse groups have painted their dreams, disappointments, and demands for change, from women's rights to LGBTQ+ activism, environmental causes to economic fairness.

In Richmond, there were ardent advocates of the women's suffrage movement. Women in Richmond started organizing in the early 1900s as the national discourse around women's voting rights picked up steam. In 1909, the Equal Suffrage League of Virginia was established to promote women's voting rights. The 19th Amendment was ratified in 1920 as a result of their lobbying, marches, and educational initiatives. Black women were frequently marginalized in the Richmond movement, as they were in many other Southern cities, and they would go on to struggle for racial equality and voting rights at the same time.

Richmond experienced a growth in environmental advocacy in the second half of the 20th century. The James River, a well-known landmark, became the focus of these initiatives. Ecosystems there were threatened by pollution brought on by industrial expansion. The river and the ecosystem it surrounded were cleaned up, preserved, and protected by grass-roots organizations. Their activism resulted in more stringent environmental laws and raised community understanding of the value of conservation.

At the same time, the labor movement in Richmond grew, especially in the years following World War II. Workers started organizing for higher pay, safer working conditions, and job security in a variety of sectors, from manufacturing to public services. Picket lines and strikes began to represent the class conflicts in Richmond, highlighting the enormous economic inequities and promoting more just economic policies.

The LGBTQ+ community in Richmond made tremendous advancements over the last half of the 20th century as well. Underground clubs and private gatherings served as safe havens during the early days, which were characterized by secrecy and fear. Even though it was devastating, the AIDS crisis in the 1980s inspired advocacy and enhanced community awareness. Richmond has developed throughout time to accommodate Pride celebrations and LGBTQ+ organizations, establishing a more inclusive and welcoming atmosphere.

At the turn of the 2000, Richmond was struggling with its complicated past. Confederate monument-related movements that call for their removal or reinterpretation gained popularity. These discussions included a range of topics, including dealing with historical narratives, comprehending the effects of racism, and identifying the images and narratives that best reflected the city.

Chapter 17: Technological Revolution of the 20th Century to the Millennium

Technology advanced at an unprecedented rate throughout the second half of the 20th century, substantially changing all facets of daily life. With its historical roots and changing urban environment, Richmond was able to both influence and profit from these transitional periods.

Like much of America, Richmond started to experience the tremendous effects of television as the post-World War II age came into being. In Richmond, television ownership increased dramatically in the 1950s, making them the mainstays of family entertainment. Local broadcasters increased their audience by offering a mix of national and local programs on stations like WRVA-TV (now WWBT). Television changed more than simply entertainment; it also affected how Richmonders got their news, participated in politics, and even went shopping, with commercials becoming a common cultural phenomena.

With the development of computer technology, another big change occurred in the 1960s and 1970s. Particularly in Richmond's financial and political sectors, people started to realize how useful computers could be for speeding processes and increasing accuracy. Businesses switched over to using digital databases instead of manual ledgers, while educational institutions like Virginia Commonwealth University began incorporating computer science and technology into their curricula to prepare the next generation for the digital era.

Personal computers began to enter Richmond homes and schools in the 1980s. Individuals were able to interact with computing on a personal level thanks to the democratization of technology, from word processing to the earliest varieties of online gaming. The public schools in Richmond incorporated computer literacy into their curricula to ensure that students were ready for a labor market that was changing quickly.

However, the rise of the Internet in the 1990s may have had a more profoundly altering effect on Richmond than any other technical advancement. The city connected to a worldwide network thanks to local service providers, which changed community, communication, and commerce. Digital start-ups were swiftly launched by Richmond entrepreneurs who saw the potential, and traditional firms rushed to create an online presence.

The mobile revolution began to take off towards the turn of the millennium. In the late 1980s and the early 1990s, cell phones were a luxury item, but they quickly became commonplace. By the early 2000s, these gadgets were more than simply phones; they were also tiny computers with internet browsing, emailing, and photo-taking capabilities. With this trend, the urban and suburban landscapes of Richmond changed, bringing with it an increase in vendors of tech accessories, repair facilities, and mobile service providers.

Alongside these technological changes, there occurred a cultural revolution. Significant adjustments were made to how Richmonders interacted with one another, worked, played, and shopped. With the growth of tech-related jobs, the city's economy diversified, and the connections and perspectives from across the world made possible by the Internet improved its social fabric.

Chapter 18: Changing Demographics and Culture of the 20th Century to the Millennium

In the 20th century, Richmond underwent waves of transformation that reshaped its socioeconomic structure. The city experienced substantial demographic changes as the century went on, which in turn affected its cultural and societal norms and produced a dynamic interaction between enduring traditions and developing identities.

Significant population movements started right after World War II ended. After the war, Richmond had a boom in internal migration as a result of the booming economy. Many African Americans from rural Virginia made their way to the city, drawn by the promise of an urban lifestyle and industrial prospects. With the establishment of dynamic communities that would later develop into cultural centers, this migration started to transform areas.

In the same time frame, Richmond's suburbs started to grow as a result of the national suburbanization trend. Many of Richmond's white residents could live in suburban areas while still working in the city thanks to the construction of highways and the rising cost of cars. Due to what some refer to as "white flight," the downtown sections became largely African American.

In the second half of the 20th century, Richmond also started to become more international. A wider range of immigrants were able to enter the United States thanks to the Immigration and Nationality Act of 1965, which did away with tight immigration quotas. Immigrants from Latin America, Asia, and Africa began to arrive in Richmond steadily. With their unique cultures, traditions, and cuisines, these populations added layers to Richmond's already rich fabric, resulting in regions of the city that reflect international influences.

A younger demographic started settling in Richmond as a result of the growth of educational institutions like Virginia Commonwealth University in the later part of the century. Students from all over the nation and the world revitalized some areas of the city by bringing with them fresh perspectives, artistic expression, and musical talent. As the population changed, new festivals, art galleries, music venues, and unique restaurants started to appear.

A cultural transformation occurred together with these population changes. Richmond was profoundly affected by the Civil Rights Movement of the 1960s and 1970s, which demanded equality and questioned traditional conventions. Reflections on the city's involvement in the Confederacy led to analyses of its historical narratives and monuments.

In Richmond, as well as other progressive groups, the voices of the women's liberation movement, the LGBTQ+ rights movement, and others could be heard. The city started embracing a future of inclusivity and diversity while still respecting its past.

Chapter 19: Post-9/11 Richmond

In Richmond, the morning of September 11, 2001, was no different from any other. However, the city's rhythm was disrupted when word of the terrorist assaults on the World Trade Center and the Pentagon spread. In offices, petrol stations, and public spaces, people gathered around televisions. Every inhabitant was shocked by the tragedy's scope, which served as a reminder of even the most resilient communities' fragility.

Due to its proximity to Washington, D.C., Richmond experienced a noticeable tension. Security was tightened up, particularly around historical monuments, transit hubs, and governmental facilities. It became routine to see more military and police presence. Businesses closed early, parents rushed to schools to pick up their kids, and a gloomy atmosphere pervaded the city.

However, amid the early shock and loss, a stronger than ever sense of community formed. For those looking for comfort and understanding, churches, mosques, synagogues, and other houses of worship opened their doors. There were organized vigils and memorial events that attracted people from various backgrounds. Long queues could be seen at blood drives, and community outreach initiatives worked nonstop to help people who were directly or indirectly impacted.

Like many other American communities, Richmond struggled in the weeks and months that followed with the effects of 9/11's economic fallout. The initial fear of traveling had an impact on tourism, a crucial industry for the city, which is famed for its ancient landmarks. Local companies felt the squeeze, particularly those involved in the tourism and hospitality industries.

However, Richmond also evaluated its identity during this era of reflection. Discussions regarding what it means to be an American, the variety of the country, and the value of unity in diversity became more prominent. The Civil War and the Civil Rights Movement divisions that frequently defined the city's rich past served as a touchstone for these conversations.

Richmond's educational institutions were crucial in promoting conversation. Universities and schools evolved become forums for discussion, comprehension, and education. More recent global events were included in the curriculum, fostering a more complex view of world affairs.

Civic initiatives started prior to 9/11 took on new significance after the attacks. The effort to revitalize Richmond's downtown was seen as more than just a business venture; it was also seen as a testament to the city's resiliency and forward motion.

Richmond saw a cultural boom that produced works of literature and art that were timely. Loss, identity, and optimism were topics that singers, authors, and artists struggled with. Art galleries, theaters, and performance spaces in the city served as vital sites for processing societal pain and imagining a better future.

The raw wounds of 9/11 started to fade as the years progressed into decades, but the memories persisted. The events of that dreadful day and its aftermath added another painful, resilient, and enduringly communal chapter to Richmond's lengthy history.

Chapter 20: Contemporary Challenges and Opportunities

After 9/11, Richmond through a journey of resiliency and reflection, but as it advanced into the twenty-first century, new opportunities and difficulties appeared. Richmond was under pressure to change and remake itself as the economy shifted from one based on industry to one that was centered on technology, healthcare, and services.

The decline of Richmond's once-dominant industrial sector led to job losses and the requirement for workforce retraining. Without ignoring its vulnerable citizens, the city had to face the difficulties of modernization. The need to address these socioeconomic changes grew. Initiatives to improve digital literacy, career training in developing industries, and assistance for small enterprises were prioritized.

Richmond experienced both economic and environmental difficulties. Cities like Richmond find themselves at the nexus of urban expansion and sustainable living as a result of rising global temperatures. Growing concern was being expressed about the health of the James River and the city's parks. Investments in green building projects, better public transit options, and river cleanup campaigns were made possible by this resurging environmental conscience.

The population of Richmond changed, becoming more varied, bringing with it a variety of cultures, views, and aspirations. Although this diversity was valued, it also presented difficulties. It became crucial to make sure that all communities felt represented and had equal access to opportunities. Through festivals, exhibitions, and educational initiatives, efforts were made to strengthen community engagement, enhance public services in minority communities, and celebrate the rich tapestry of cultures.

But chances also came with difficulties. The city of Richmond's expanding cultural scene became a popular destination for both visitors and locals. The city, which was already well-known for its historical sites, began to gain popularity for its modern art galleries, music events, and culinary scene. The crowded hubs of Silicon Valley and New York started to be oversaturated, and Richmond started to be seen as a desirable alternative. Local institutions served as talent pools and think tanks for startups, creating a welcoming environment.

Innovative solutions were also required to address the problems of urban sprawl and cheap housing. Commercial and residential spaces coexisted in revitalized downtown areas, enhancing walkability and cutting down on travel time. There were campaigns to promote more community gardens, green rooftops, and pedestrian-friendly areas.

Despite this, Richmond's past continued to serve as a guide for its goals for the future. Lessons learned from its past—both happy and sad—served as reminders of the necessity for growth, equity, and inclusion. The city's historical sites evolved into hubs for conversation and instruction, fusing historical accounts with cutting-edge debates.

Richmond navigated the complexity of the twenty-first century with an understanding of its difficulties and a clear sense of the opportunities they offered. Richmond aimed to be a city of the future, based on the pillars of its past, while embracing change and remaining rooted in its identity.

Chapter 21: Famous Personalities from Richmond

Numerous people who have made irrevocable contributions to the history and culture of the country were either born in Richmond or called it their home.

The renowned tennis player and humanitarian Arthur Ashe was a Richmond native. He broke through barriers on the court and off it by being the first African American to take home a Grand Slam title. In addition to his athletic talent, Ashe was a vocal advocate for civil rights and worked to end apartheid in South Africa.

Another notable Richmonder was influential novelist Ellen Glasgow. Her writings examined early 20th-century socioeconomic developments while delving deeply into the Southern mind. She won the Pulitzer Prize for Literature in 1942 thanks to her astute assessments of gender roles and social strata.

Maggie L. Walker, a pioneer in finance, is a well-known Richmond resident. She broke through barriers in even the most male-dominated industries by becoming the first Black woman to charter a bank in the United States. In the city's Jackson Ward area, formerly referred to as "Harlem of the South," her influence is still felt today.

Author and historian Douglas Southall Freeman offered in-depth analyses of the Civil War and its leading players. He was awarded two Pulitzer Prizes for his multi-volume works on George Washington and Robert E. Lee. For those researching the Civil War era, Freeman's publications are essential—though oftentimes contentious—reading because of his in-depth and frequently sympathetic portrayal of the Confederacy.

The Grammy-winning musician Aimee S. Mann spent her formative years in Richmond. She has become a significant character in the alternative rock and folk genres thanks to her moving lyrics and heartfelt music.

Warren Beatty is a renowned actor in both theater and movies. Beatty, a Richmond native, has had a distinguished career as an actor, director, and producer. He has received multiple Academy Award nominations. His movies, like "Bonnie and Clyde" and "Reds," have permanently altered Hollywood.

Another notable Richmond resident was the renowned tap dancer Bill "Bojangles" Robinson. He popularized tap dancing and rose to fame on both the stage and in movies. His attempts to break down racial boundaries and his contributions to the arts have solidified his legacy.

These people have roots in Richmond's soil, along with many more. They have moved around the intricate terrain of the city, taking inspiration from its people, struggles, and stories. By doing this, they have not only established their own reputations but also raised the status of a city whose residents continue to be inspired by, challenged by, and shaped by it.

Chapter 22: Richmond as Seen on TV

When Richmond's cinematic appeal is taken into account, it's no surprise that numerous TV shows and movies have found inspiration there, using the city's diverse architecture and landscapes to set the scene for storylines in a variety of genres.

The 2012 film "Lincoln" by Steven Spielberg is among the most notable mentions. Despite being a movie rather than a TV show, it had a significant impact. The majority of this Academy Award-winning movie was filmed in Richmond. In place of the U.S. Capitol, the Virginia State Capitol served as the backdrop, while the city's historic streets and structures served as an accurate representation of Washington, D.C. in the 1860s.

Richmond was featured in the "TURN: Washington's Spies" AMC television series. The program used a number of places in and around Richmond to represent the world of espionage in the 18th century, including the famous Shirley Plantation and the streets of Petersburg. It told the narrative of America's first spy ring during the Revolutionary War.

The biographical movie "Harriet," about Harriet Tubman, introduced Cynthia Erivo to the scenery of Virginia. This moving account of one of America's most well-known freedom fighters additional dimension thanks to several Richmond sites.

Richmond became the setting for the post-apocalyptic "The Walking Dead: World Beyond" scenario. The series, a spinoff of the well-known "The Walking Dead," used the city's urban and suburban areas to film scenes and create its creepy, post-apocalyptic atmosphere.

The acclaimed HBO miniseries "John Adams" made the most of Virginia's historic locations from the colonial and Revolutionary Wars.

The city of Richmond and its surroundings served as a stand-in for numerous foreign sites, such as Philadelphia and even regions of Europe.

"Homeland," a more modern show that spent most of its final seasons in Virginia, frequently used Richmond's urban and suburban landscapes to depict both domestic and foreign places, adding to the story's tense moments.

Beyond these well-known productions, Richmond has been in a plethora of other works, including independent movies and documentaries. Each performance, in its own unique way, featured various elements of the city, from its charming history to its vibrant present.

Locals frequently felt a sense of pride when they saw their favorite city on television. These images acted as an invitation to the rest of the world, enticing them to discover Richmond's richness and depth, beyond what is merely produced and staged.

Chapter 23: Richmond as Depicted in Literature

Richmond has long served as a source of inspiration for authors, poets, and novelists because of its historical significance and cultural diversity. Numerous authors, including those from far and near, have immortalized the city's complex story in their works, which have appeared on countless pages.

Richmond society of the 1930s is skillfully explored in Ellen Glasgow's Pulitzer Prize–winning novel, "In This Our Life." Glasgow offers a thorough look into the social fabric of Richmond, stressing the racial and class tensions that were evident at the period via the lens of two sisters and their divergent destinies.

Despite being more frequently linked to Baltimore, Edgar Allan Poe actually spent a significant amount of his youth in Richmond. His complex relationship with the city is evident in pieces like "To Helen" and "A Dream Within a Dream." The undercurrents of his experiences in the city are apparent in his evocative style and melancholy tone, even though Richmond isn't explicitly mentioned.

In addition to being a pleasant exploration of Southern quirkiness, T.R. Pearson's "A Short History of a Small Place" also serves as a subliminal critique of major cities like Richmond through his depiction of small-town Virginia. Even if they are overdone, the comedy and eccentricities appeal to people who are familiar with Richmond's oddities.

Given Richmond's role as the capital of the Confederacy, the Civil War has served as the setting for several books. Richmond is mentioned multiple times in the classic novel "Gone with the Wind" by Margaret Mitchell, highlighting its significance during the turbulent wartime years. Michael Shaara's "The Killer Angels" is another powerful composition. While the Battle of Gettysburg is the main focus, Richmond's strategic and symbolic importance is often emphasized.

Tom Robbins, a well-known name in American literature, was raised in Richmond but was born at Blowing Rock, North Carolina. His book "Even Cowgirls Get the Blues" contains multiple references to the metropolis. Robbins incorporates references to Richmond throughout the protagonist's journey to show the impact the city had on him when he was a young man.

"Jacob's Ladder: A Story of Virginia During the War" by Donald McCaig pays literary homage to the James River, one of Richmond's distinctive topographical features. The James River plays a significant role in the lives of those around as the story develops against the backdrop of the Civil War, nearly taking on the role of a character.

It is clear that Richmond left a significant literary legacy. There is no disputing the city's impact on literature, whether it be as a location, a silent muse, or a representation of more important ideas. Readers can learn about different aspects of Richmond through each of these stories, which highlight the city's complexity, charm, and ever-changing character.

Chapter 24: Iconic Richmond Landmarks and History

The Virginia State Capitol is arguably Richmond's most pronounced icon. This neoclassical wonder, created by Thomas Jefferson and Charles-Louis Clérisseau, was finished in 1788. The Capitol is a historical archive in addition to being a work of art in architecture. It has been the hub of Virginia's political life for centuries and served as the Confederacy's capital during the American Civil War.

Monument Avenue, which for a long time served as a tribute to the Confederacy's leading individuals, is located not far from the Capitol. The disputes surrounding these statues and their significance over time have caused a reevaluation of the avenue's history, reflecting the city's changing perspective on its past.

One of the most well-known writers in America is honored at the Edgar Allan Poe Museum. This museum, which is housed in Richmond's oldest still-standing mansion, provides insights into Poe's time in the city by showcasing his life and creative output.

The James River plays a significant role in Richmond's history. One of the most important iron foundries in the South was The Tredegar Iron Works, which was located on its banks. It played a crucial role in creating artillery for the Confederacy during the American Civil War. The American Civil War Museum now resides there, delving deeply into the conflict's tales from all angles.

The Hollywood Cemetery, another treasure, is a serene resting spot with views of the James River. James Monroe, John Tyler, and Jefferson Davis, as well as the president of the Confederacy, are all buried there; it was founded in 1847. Its winding walks, which are lined with Gothic and

Victorian structures, offer a tranquil setting in which to consider the city's complex past.

Despite its unassuming exterior, St. John's Church played a significant role in America's journey toward independence. Patrick Henry made his stirring "Give me liberty, or give me death!" speech here in 1775, which became a rallying cry for the colonies.

Dedicated to honoring the life of a groundbreaking African American woman, Maggie L. Walker National Historic Site. Maggie Walker's home is a testimony to her tenacity and vision in the face of racial and gender biases as the first woman to charter a bank in the United States.

The Black History Museum and Cultural Center of Virginia must be mentioned in any analysis of Richmond's landmarks. The museum, which is located in the historic Leigh Street Armory, explores the diverse history of African American experiences, from the gloomy era of slavery to their tremendous achievements in the fields of the arts, politics, and civil rights.

Chapter 25: Architecture of Richmond

Richmond's architecture is an entrancing fusion of the past and the present, from the cobblestone streets of Shockoe Bottom to the modernist façade of the Museum District. Whether it be a contemporary building or a centuries-old house, every building in Richmond recounts a different chapter of the city's history, resulting in a cityscape that is as varied and vibrant as its inhabitants.

Let's start with the Virginia State Capitol, which was created by Thomas Jefferson and Charles-Louis Clérisseau. This French ancient Roman Maison Carrée-inspired neoclassical masterpiece pays homage to it with its portico's free-standing columns. Its design, which deviated from the conventional colonial style and announced a new architectural vision for America, was revolutionary for its day.

The Jefferson Hotel is a stunning example of Beaux-Arts design and another well-known building. Its magnificent design, sweeping staircase, and fine workmanship symbolize the wealth of the Gilded Age and were unveiled in 1895. Its opulent appeal is attested to by the stories that claim alligators formerly lived in its marble pools.

The majestic mansions that line Monument Avenue are examples of a variety of architectural styles. These homes, which range in style from Tudor Revival to Colonial Revival to Spanish Colonial, provide a window into the preferences and aspirations of Richmond's aristocracy in the late 19th and early 20th centuries.

Numerous Georgian and Federal-style houses may be seen in Richmond's Church Hill district, which is also where the historic St. John's Church is located. With their brick exteriors, gable roofs, and symmetrical forms, these structures transport onlookers to the city's early years. The actual church where Patrick Henry gave his well-known speech is a stunning example of Georgian colonial architecture.

Former industrial hubs and trading terminals, the Shockoe Slip and Shockoe Bottom areas have evolved into thriving urban hubs. Old warehouses have been converted into chic lofts, eateries, and boutiques in this area. Their original brickwork and big, airy windows are examples of 19th-century industrial design.

The Markel Building on West Broad Street is in sharp contrast. The round, aluminum-clad building, which resembles a baked potato wrapped in foil, was created by architect Haig Jamgochian and finished in 1965, reflecting the avant-garde, experimental style of the time.

The new additions to Richmond's Virginia Museum of Fine Arts serve as an example of modern architecture. The 2010 McGlothlin Wing is a seamless blend of glass, metal, and stone, created by Rick Mather and SMBW Architects. It stands for Richmond's aptitude for blending its illustrious architectural past with forward-thinking ideals.

Chapter 26: Key Industries of Economic Evolution

Tobacco can be credited with bringing Richmond's industrial era to a close. Because Virginia's rich soil was ideal for growing tobacco, Richmond quickly became an important center in the 18th and 19th centuries. The development of tobacco warehouses, the James River, and the Kanawha Canal helped the city become well-known in the domestic and international tobacco trade.

Similar to how tobacco became an important part of Richmond's economy, so did wheat milling. Utilizing the water power provided by the James River, mills like the Haxall Mill produced flour that was not only used domestically but also exported to foreign markets.

The importance of ironworks started to increase as the 19th century went on, with the Tredegar Iron Works taking center stage. This facility rose to prominence as one of the country's top producers of iron and artillery by the mid-1800s, especially during the Civil War, solidifying Richmond's status as an industrial powerhouse.

Richmond's industry diversified as the reconstruction era spread across the country after the Civil War. The foundations of banking and finance were laid, with organizations like the First National Bank of Richmond directing the future trajectory of the city's economy. By the turn of the 20th century, Richmond had solidified its position as the Southern United States' financial hub.

A new era of manufacturing likewise began in the 20th century. Names like Philip Morris began to be associated with Richmond, evoking its tobacco heritage in a more contemporary, industrial way. Richmond's economic character was broadened by the presence of such industrial behemoths, adding layers of complexity and dynamism.

The late 20th and early 21st centuries saw the emergence of technology and healthcare as key industries. Richmond underwent a transformation into a center for healthcare and medical research with the founding and expansion of Virginia Commonwealth University. In the meantime, Richmond was positioned as a city prepared to enter the digital age thanks to the rise of the IT industry, which was supported by established giants and spurred by entrepreneurs.

The real estate and tourism industries both grew. Richmond became a popular tourist destination as a result of its extensive history, which spans from colonial periods to Civil War battlegrounds. The city's skyline and demography were simultaneously altered by a flourishing real estate market that was driven by both residential and commercial interests.

These important industries have shaped Richmond's trajectory, which is evidence of its resiliency and adaptability. The city has continually remade itself, from the 18th-century water-powered mills to the 21st-century computer firms, guaranteeing its relevance and vitality in a constantly changing economic environment.

Chapter 27: Richmond in the National and Global Economy

The economic development of Richmond has been marked by innovation, resilience, and flexibility. Richmond's influence in the domestic and international economies is substantial and diverse, ranging from its beginnings as a trading centre in the colonial era to its current position as a hub for banking, technology, and industry.

In the past, Richmond was a thriving center for the trading of tobacco. Tobacco was more easily transported to foreign markets because to the James River, which meanders through the city. The development of flour mills and ironworks, particularly the Tredegar Iron Works, which was crucial to the Civil War, occurred in Richmond as the 19th century went on.

Heavy industry began to decline in the 20th century. By picking Richmond as their home location, various banking institutions helped Richmond develop into a financial powerhouse. like instance, the region is home to significant operations like SunTrust Banks and Capital One. This banking boom elevated Richmond to the status of one of the Southern United States' leading financial centers, supporting the city's economy and generating thousands of employment.

Richmond's economy extends beyond the banking industry. There are several Fortune 500 companies based in the city. Richmond serves as the corporate headquarters for Philip Morris USA's parent business, Altria Group. The existence of this tobacco powerhouse is a reminder to Richmond's earlier connections to the tobacco industry. Dominion Energy, a significant player in the utilities industry, deserves special recognition for highlighting the city's diverse economic environment.

Richmond was not immune to the swift changes in the global economy that occurred in the twenty-first century, notably with the development of technology and e-commerce. Richmond's key role in the East Coast distribution network is demonstrated by Amazon's decision to locate a fulfillment facility there.

Other cornerstones of Richmond's economy include research and education. Virginia Commonwealth University (VCU) is a substantial employer in addition to being a center for higher education. The VCU Health System is well-known throughout the country and attracts medical specialists from all around the world.

Additionally essential to Richmond's economy is tourism. Each year, millions of tourists are drawn to the city by its rich tapestry of history, art, and culture. A regular stream of domestic and foreign tourists, who support the local economy, is guaranteed by historical sites, festivals, and gastronomic attractions.

Port of Virginia in Richmond acts as a bridge to international markets on the international front. It is one of the busiest ports on the Eastern Seaboard, promoting trade between the United States and other nations.

Chapter 28: Notable Companies in Richmond

The Altria Group, a company whose name is inextricably linked to Richmond's tobacco history, is in the foreground. Altria, the parent company of Philip Morris USA, is one of the biggest manufacturers and distributors of tobacco, cigarettes, and associated goods worldwide. Richmond's historical connection to the production and trading of tobacco can be seen in its presence.

Another well-known brand, not just in Richmond but across the nation, is Dominion Energy. Dominion is one of the biggest energy producers and transporters in the country, and it is essential to the operation of homes and businesses. Dominion is a monument to Richmond's forward-thinking commitment to energy and sustainability with a broad energy mix that includes solar and nuclear power.

Capital One is unique among financial institutions. Since its founding in 1988, this financial behemoth has experienced rapid growth and now provides a wide range of services, including credit cards, auto loans, and savings accounts. Although it has grown nationally and internationally, its roots in Richmond remain strong, supporting thousands of jobs there.

Another well-known company with headquarters in Richmond is Genworth Financial, which focuses on insurance, wealth management, and financial products. Genworth emphasizes the city's position as a financial centre in the Southern United States with a history extending more than a century.

Richmond is home to Universal Corporation, a major provider of leaf tobacco on a global scale. Universal's operations today cover more than 30 nations, demonstrating Richmond's global corporate reach while also paying homage to the city's tobacco-related history.

CarMax and other businesses are good examples of Richmond's expanding IT sector. CarMax's success lies in the combination of automotive sales with cutting-edge technology, providing customers with a seamless digital experience. The company is well recognized as the largest used-car reseller in the country.

Performance Food Group is noteworthy in the food arena. This enterprise, which supplies a variety of food items to restaurants, cafeterias, and vending machines, highlights the importance of Richmond in the country's food distribution system.

The depth and breadth of Richmond's financial industry are demonstrated by Markel Corporation, a diverse financial holding firm that deals with investments, reinsurance, and insurance. Markel has a history that dates back to the 1930s, and its development parallels that of the city.

Chapter 29: Visual Art and Movements in Richmond

Richmond has a rich and evolving relationship with visual art that reflects the historical complexities, cultural changes, and socio-political advancements of the city. Richmond has served as a canvas and a catalyst for both avant-garde movements and classic art genres over the years.

The Virginia Museum of Fine Arts (VMFA) is in the center of Richmond's artistic community. Over 35,000 works of art are contained in its extensive collection, which dates back over 5,000 years. The VMFA presents a broad view of world art history while also honoring Virginia's own artistic past, with collections ranging from extensive African and East Asian ones to Art Nouveau and Art Deco ones.

The abundance of 19th-century buildings in Richmond's historic neighborhoods, especially in the Fan District and Church Hill, serves as a visual reminder of the city's colorful past. Murals cover the city's streets as well; the Richmond Mural Project, which aims to commission over 100 murals from prominent artists, is responsible for many of them.

Particularly in the twenty-first century, the street art movement has grown significantly. The yearly RVA Street Art Festival has changed the city's appearance, transforming decaying structures and abandoned silos into colorful paintings that tell stories about Richmond's history, present, and potential futures.

Richmond has a thriving art education and incubation scene, with a major contribution coming from the School of the Arts at Virginia Commonwealth University (VCUarts). Emerging artists have flourished at VCUarts, one of the top art schools in the country, and many of them have opted to remain in Richmond, enhancing the city's art culture.

Richmond's art scene is notable for its participation in socio-political discussions. Civil rights, equality, and justice are some of the subjects that Richmond artists have addressed over the years. Particularly in light of the Black Lives Matter movement, the Confederate monuments that once dominated Monument Avenue became focal centers of creative and political expression. These sculptures were transformed into moving protest and contemplation canvases by temporary installations, graffiti, and projections.

Contemporary artists can display their work in galleries like 1708 Gallery and Quirk Gallery, which frequently blur the distinctions between conventional art forms and cutting-edge mediums. The diverse artistic community in Richmond has a voice thanks to pop-up exhibitions, artist collectives, and collaborative events that reflect a wide range of backgrounds, ideologies, and aspirations.

Richmond has seen a lot of grassroots art movements that have developed out of the stories and needs of the locals. The city's art trends are as diverse as they are lively, from the tattoo renaissance that saw Richmond become a national center for tattoo art to the folk art traditions rooted in Virginia's Appalachian roots.

Chapter 30: Music and Musical Movements in Richmond

In Richmond, musical revolutions have been spawned, fostered, and celebrated over the years. Richmond has served as a melodic cauldron where classical symphonies and grassroots punk collide.

Institutions like the Richmond Symphony Orchestra have served as the foundation of the city's classical scene. Since its founding in 1957, it has provided Richmond citizens with the best symphonic music available, ranging from Beethoven symphonies to modern works that represent both the timeless classics and the developing sensibilities of a new age.

Jazz has a long history in Richmond as well. Midway through the 20th century, Jackson Ward—often referred to as the "Harlem of the South"—became the core of the city's burgeoning jazz culture. Legendary performers like Duke Ellington and Ella Fitzgerald have performed in Richmond, forever influencing the city's musical culture.

Without discussing Richmond's thriving punk and metal scenes, one cannot talk about the city's musical tapestry. The 1980s and 1990s were pivotal years for music, with underground acts finding a stage at places like 929 West Grace Street. In Richmond, the DIY movement flourished, giving rise to important punk, hardcore, and metal bands like GWAR and Avail.

In parallel with the noisier genres, Richmond became the center of the indie rock movement. Bands like Lucy Dacus and Lamb of God perfectly capture the city's varied rock soundscape, which draws inspiration from heavy metal to folk.

Rap and hip-hop have also carved out a sizable space in Richmond's musical environment. Richmond has been represented nationally by artists like Mad Skillz and Michael Millions, who combine incisive poetry with heartfelt observations of daily life.

Festivals like the RVA Jazz Festival and Friday Cheers on Brown's Island, which draw large crowds and feature a mix of local performers and international names, have developed into city traditions. Such occasions have enhanced Richmond's standing as a place where music is truly alive and well.

The next generation of musicians has been fostered by organizations like the Department of Music at Virginia Commonwealth University (VCU), which provides a mix of classical instruction and modern methods. In particular, VCU's jazz studies program pays homage to Richmond's long jazz history.

Chapter 31: Other Cultural Festivals in Richmond

One such occasion that has a particularly strong impact on city dwellers is the Richmond Folk Festival. An annual celebration of the origins, depth, and diversity of American culture, it takes place along Richmond's famed downtown waterfront. It is one of the most anticipated festivals in the city and features music, dance, crafts, and food from various cultural communities. This festival attracts tens of thousands of tourists each year.

One other important event in Richmond's cultural calendar is the Dominion Energy Riverrock festival. Although it is largely recognized as the best outdoor music and sports event on the East Coast, its cultural significance should not be disregarded. This festival, which is set against the background of the James River and blends musical performances with art and athletic competitions, embodies the city's appreciation of the great outdoors and its thriving cultural community.

The Asian American Celebration honors the growing Asian community in Richmond. This festival, which is held every year, has performances, food stands, crafts, and exhibits from countries ranging from the Middle East to the Far East, showcasing the diverse tapestry of Asian cultures.

Richmond's cultural environment gives Cinco de Mayo a distinct position as a reflection of the city's expanding Hispanic population. While the event is a celebration of the triumph of the Mexican Army over the French Empire, it is also a large-scale celebration of Hispanic culture in Richmond, complete with parades, music, dancing, and food.

The French Film Festival is a celebration of Richmond's international flair and is held by the Byrd Theatre. This festival celebrates French cinema in all its splendour, from avant-garde experimentation to box office successes, by showcasing the most recent works from France's best directors.

On the other side, the Richmond International Film Festival (RIFF) brings world film to the city's doorsteps. RIFF, a confluence of creation that brings together movie screenings, musical performances, and industry panels, attracts artists and creators from all over the world.

In Richmond, the Juneteenth Festival honors African American ancestry. The event, which honors the abolition of slavery in the United States, combines historical commemoration with cultural celebration. It features music, dance, and storytelling sessions that are strongly rooted in the culture and history of the city.

The Hanover Tomato Festival, which honors the prized tomatoes of the area, is a somewhat eccentric addition to Richmond's cultural offerings. What started as a modest celebration of the tomato has grown into a large-scale event featuring entertainment, arts and crafts, rides, and, of course, tomatoes in every imaginable culinary form.

Chapter 32: Key Educational Institutions

The diversity and excellence of the city's schools and institutions demonstrate its dedication to education.

Without a doubt, Virginia Commonwealth University (VCU) is one of the most well-known. VCU, which is located in the center of Richmond, is famous for both its broad selection of academic programs and its vibrant campus culture. The university's School of the Arts is regularly named as one of the top schools in the nation, and its health sciences departments, in particular the VCU Medical Center, are essential to healthcare teaching and research.

Another school that has permanently altered the academic fabric of the city is University of Richmond (UR). UR has a beautiful campus that encircles Westhampton Lake and offers a demanding liberal arts curriculum. Particularly renowned are the Robins School of Business and School of Law, which have produced numerous generations of business and legal professionals.

The historically black university, Virginia Union University (VUU), is a shining example of this. VUU, which was initially established soon after the Civil War to give newly freed slaves access to educational possibilities, has grown into a complete institution. While VUU's departments in theology and religious studies are particularly noteworthy, its overall commitment to social justice and community leadership penetrates every aspect of its curriculum.

With a more adaptable educational style, Reynolds Community College serves both regular students and those looking for continuing education or occupational training. As one of Virginia's biggest community colleges, Reynolds is essential to ensuring that all facets of Richmond's population have access to and value from higher education.

Richmond is also proud of its strong K–12 educational system. The city's dedication to fostering young talent is demonstrated by the existence of the Maggie L. Walker Governor's School for Government and International Studies. As a magnet school, it enrolls gifted kids from all around the area and provides them with a rigorous curriculum that places an emphasis on civic involvement, global studies, and leadership.

Benedictine College Preparatory provides an all-male, Catholic military high school education with a focus on discipline, honor, and leadership for individuals wanting an education with a strong religious foundation. Similar to St. Catherine's School, which promotes academic excellence within an Episcopal context, is an all-female alternative.

From junior kindergarten through high school, St. Christopher's School, a partner institution of St. Catherine's, provides an all-male learning environment. The institution has been a mainstay in Richmond's educational scene thanks to its illustrious history and dedication to developing well-rounded students.

Chapter 33: Richmond's Role in Academia and Research

While Richmond is rich in history and culture, it has also quietly but persistently established itself as a center for learning and research across many different fields. Institutions in the city have significantly influenced the larger academic community by producing innovations and scientific achievements that have attracted both domestic and international attention.

Virginia Commonwealth University (VCU) is essential to Richmond's academic reputation. Beyond its dedication to superior teaching, VCU is a major player in the field of research. In particular, the VCU Medical Center is in the vanguard of developments in healthcare and medicine. It has played a key role in developing research on numerous diseases and medical technology thanks to its cutting-edge facilities. Its initiatives in the fields of cardiology, neurology, and organ transplantation are particularly noteworthy and have attracted researchers and medical professionals from all over the world.

Additionally, the VCU School of Engineering has been a pioneer in cutting-edge technical study. The School of Engineering has made significant contributions in fields ranging from innovative manufacturing methods to sustainable energy solutions that go far beyond Richmond's city limits.

Interdisciplinary studies have a strong academic heritage at the University of Richmond. Although it provides a wide range of study opportunities, it has made notably significant contributions to sustainability and environmental studies. The UR Environmental Studies program frequently works on projects that combine policy analysis with scientific research, giving insights on both regional ecologies and worldwide environmental trends.

With its illustrious past, Virginia Union University (VUU) has a special place in academic studies on African American history, religion, and social justice. Scholars and historians have benefited greatly from the institution's extensive study into the African diaspora, civil rights, and the overall African American experience.

Richmond also features a number of specialized research institutes and think tanks. The significant history of the state has been preserved and studied in large part by the Virginia Historical Society. It offers a thorough insight into Virginia's past through its extensive archives, exhibitions, and publications, making it an essential tool for historians, students, and enthusiasts alike.

Another notable asset to Richmond's intellectual environment is the Science Museum of Virginia. Although its primary purpose is to educate the general public, it also performs significant research in areas like astronomy, paleontology, and environmental science.

The expansion of Richmond as a corporate center has sparked research and development across a range of industries in the private sector. The city's biotech, IT, and entrepreneurs focused on sustainable energy have been driving research to meet demands and markets around the world.

Chapter 34: Natural Disasters in Richmond and their Impact

Richmond is situated at a special confluence of natural forces due to its geographic location. The city enjoys beautiful scenery thanks to this convergence, but it has also become more vulnerable to numerous natural calamities over time. The infrastructure and regulations of the city have been greatly influenced by these occurrences, but also the community spirit and resiliency of the city as a whole.

Historically, Richmond has faced a significant natural disaster threat from hurricanes. Since the city is inland, it doesn't experience the full force of these storms like coastal towns do, but the aftershocks are still felt strongly. Flooding is a common hurricane aftereffect, especially along the James River. For instance, Hurricane Isabel in 2003 caused considerable floods, widespread power outages, uprooted trees, and extensive property damage.

For many locals, the memories of Tropical Storm Gaston from 2004 is still fresh. By the time it hit Richmond, it had not yet developed into a hurricane, but the damage it caused was severe. Particularly Richmond's downtown experienced significant floods. Shockoe Bottom, with its shops, landmarks, and homes, was severely flooded, resulting in enormous financial losses and the eviction of numerous residents.

Although less common, tornadoes have also made an appearance in Richmond. Over the years, there have been numerous tornado warnings for the city and its neighboring counties, some of which have caused property damage, uprooted trees, and power outages.

Flooding is still a constant issue, frequently made worse by hurricanes and a lot of rain. Richmond's signature river, the James, has occasionally overflowed its banks, affecting nearby communities and forcing evacuations. To lessen these threats, efforts have been made to erect safety barriers and keep the river flowing.

Blizzards and winter storms are another aspect of Richmond's history with natural disasters. Even though snow gives the city a lovely coating, it frequently causes problems with traffic, power outages, and infrastructure damage.

These natural disasters have an effect that goes beyond just the immediate harm they cause to infrastructure and property. Richmond has been financially hit hard by shut down companies, repair expenses, and disrupted services. The issues of post-disaster restoration and community displacement have been observed socially in the city.

But despite these difficulties, Richmond's spirit has prevailed. The neighborhood has repeatedly banded together to repair, help those who were harmed, and learn from each incident. With investments in infrastructure, early warning systems, and community preparedness initiatives, the city's disaster response procedures have developed with each disaster.

While difficult, natural calamities have shown Richmond's resiliency and solidarity. They served as striking reminders of nature's erratic might while also showcasing Richmonders' unflappable spirit. Richmond has overcome these obstacles with tenacity and elegance because to community efforts, policy changes, and a firm dedication to preserving its history and populace.

Chapter 35: History of Sports and Athletes from Richmond

The rise of teams, memorable moments, and star athletes are all part of Richmond's rich and varied athletic legacy. The city's passion of athletics is ingrained in its culture, and it has made numerous, major contributions to the larger athletic community.

Richmond's heartbeat has long been centered upon baseball. Over the years, the city has hosted a number of minor league teams, and many players have passed through on their route to become major league stars. With numerous historic seasons and rising stars, the Richmond Braves, the Triple-A affiliate of the Atlanta Braves for more than 40 years, were a significant part of the city's baseball history. The Richmond Flying Squirrels, the San Francisco Giants' Double-A club, have recently won the hearts of the people by providing thrilling games and a sense of community.

Richmond has experienced a rise in popularity and success for basketball. Basketball programs at Virginia Commonwealth University (VCU) and the University of Richmond both have a rich history. With its Cinderella story run to the NCAA Final Four in 2011, VCU in particular garnered media attention, enhancing the city's standing as a basketball mecca.

There are a number of well-known individual athletes from Richmond. Tennis prodigy Arthur Ashe, a city native, broke multiple barriers in the game by playing as an African American in a largely white sport and by engaging in classy activism off the field. The Arthur Ashe Athletic Center and a significant statue on Monument Avenue honor his legacy in the city.

Richmond has witnessed a rise in the popularity of American football, particularly since the Washington Football Team has set up camp there.

Richmond's position in the larger American football landscape has been cemented as a result of this, which has also brought an influx of supporters and tourists.

The James River, which plays a crucial role in Richmond in many ways, has served as the setting for a variety of water sports and events. Making the most of the river's tough currents and natural beauty, rowing contests, kayaking, and other water sports have become more and more popular.

Richmond is known to NASCAR fans for the Richmond Raceway, which has hosted prestigious stock car races for many years. Many Richmonders look forward to the thunder of engines and the thrilling atmosphere on race weekends.

The Richmond Kickers are a stalwart in the world of soccer, helping to develop the game and inspiring supporters of all ages with their spirit of competition.

Richmond's sports landscape is as varied as its past, from ballparks and basketball courts to the screaming racetrack and the peaceful James River. Along with producing elite athletes, the city has fostered a passion for sports that unites its residents, recognizes its triumphs, and perseveres in the face of adversity. The reverberating cheers, the shared triumphs and tragedies, and the tales of physical skill are all significant chapters in Richmond's lengthy narrative.

Chapter 36: Noteworthy Recreational Spaces

The James River Park System is among the most famous public places. This vast natural refuge offers a variety of activities and stretches for kilometers along the James River. It's a diverse location, offering tranquil fishing holes in addition to the class III and IV rapids that entice kayakers and white-water rafters. Hikers, joggers, and mountain bikers all enjoy the park's trails, such as the North Bank and Buttermilk Trails, for their scenic beauty and difficult terrain.

A 100-acre Victorian estate called Maymont offers a unique synthesis of nature and history. In addition to its historic mansion, Maymont has a children's farm, Japanese and Italian gardens, and a display of local wildlife. Maymont is a well-liked destination for relaxation and family vacations, whether you're strolling around themed gardens or having a picnic on its vast grounds.

Another treasure is the 287-acre Byrd Park. The park is a well-liked location for fishing and paddle boating because to its three lakes, Fountain Lake, Swan Lake, and Shields Lake. Those looking for an athletic workout amidst nature can take advantage of The Vita Course, a fitness trail.

Monroe Park, located in the center of the city, is a haven from the metropolis. As Richmond's oldest park, it has undergone a number of modifications to maintain its charm and meet contemporary recreational demands. It is a well-liked location for students, families, and events thanks to its center fountain, historical monuments, and plenty of open space.

The richness of nature is displayed in the Lewis Ginter Botanical Garden. The garden, which covers 50 acres, features numerous plant collections.

The themed gardens, including the Children's Garden and the Rose Garden, as well as the domed conservatory, which houses exotic plants, are highlights.

The recreation area and historical site Belle Isle are situated in Richmond. Visitors are treated to hiking and bike routes, rock climbing options, and expansive views of the river and city skyline, all of which are accessible through a pedestrian bridge. Visitors are reminded of the island's colorful past by the ruins of former factories and the Civil War prison camp.

With its lake and undulating hills, Forest Hill Park is a tranquil haven. A weekly farmers market, hiking, and live music are currently held in the park, which was formerly a part of a sizable estate.

Chapter 37: Noteworthy Nature in Richmond

Richmond's natural beauty is a mesmerizing combination of lush surroundings, varied flora and wildlife, and a gorgeous river that has significantly influenced the development of the city's character. Richmond's surrounding natural environment is a monument to the region's significant ecological diversity and gives locals and visitors alike a chance to get in touch with nature in a crowded city.

Richmond's lifeblood, the James River, flows smoothly through the city. It is more than just a body of water; it is an ecosystem brimming with life. The James River is a dynamic habitat, home to ospreys and bald eagles soaring in the skies, as well as the resilient Atlantic sturgeon, a prehistoric fish that has made the river its spawning ground. Beavers, river otters, and even the occasional deer can be found living along the riverbanks among the rich greenery.

The trees in Richmond contribute significantly to the city's green image while remaining silently present. The urban environment and the nearby parks are covered in tall tulip poplars, oaks, and hickories, many of which have been standing for generations. Dogwoods and redbuds burst into flower in the spring, painting the town in a rainbow of pink, white, and purple hues.

The grounds and gardens at Maymont provide a glimpse into a variety of environments. Turtles, frogs, and a variety of birds can be seen in the area's marshes, and owls and foxes can be found on the estate's higher hills. The large Maymont grounds also include themed gardens. A window into other ecologies can be seen in the tranquil Italian Garden and the tranquil Japanese Garden with their koi-filled ponds.

For those who love plants, the Lewis Ginter Botanical Garden is a paradise. Beyond the decorative collections, this area cultivates indigenous plants to ensure the survival of the local flora and the attraction of pollinators like butterflies and hummingbirds. The conservatory at the garden provides a special contrast to the natural species of Virginia with its collection of tropical and desert plants.

Belle Isle presents a wilder side of nature with its rocky outcrops and fast waterways. The island's distinctive geological features draw adventure seekers interested in rock-hopping or up-close river rapids viewing as well as wildlife lovers.

While Richmond's parks and gardens provide planned natural experiences, untamed beauty may be found nearby in a short drive. Pocahontas State Park and the Chickahominy species Management Area in the neighborhood both offer vast landscapes with forests, ponds, and lakes that serve as habitats for a variety of species.

In Richmond, the natural world plays a more active role in the city's narrative than it does as a simple backdrop. Richmond's natural surroundings serve as a constant reminder of the delicate balance that must be maintained between urban development and environmental stewardship, whether it be the soft lapping of the James River's waters against its banks, the chirping of cicadas on a summer evening, or the rustling of autumn leaves in one of its many parks. Future generations will be able to appreciate and be inspired by Richmond's rich ecological tapestry because to the city's dedication to protecting its natural beauty.

Chapter 38: Environmental Issues in Richmond

With its blend of urban and rural surroundings, Richmond has encountered its fair share of environmental difficulties. Richmond has experienced expansion and development at the expense of the environment frequently since it is a historic city that has changed with the times. These difficulties have, however, also sparked a push toward better awareness and pro-active remedies.

The James River's water quality has long been a source of worry. For many years, sewage overflows, stormwater runoff, and industrial discharges caused excessive levels of pollution in the river. Algal blooms caused by high nutrient loads have been accompanied by toxin-induced fish population declines and ecosystem damage in the river. Despite recent major improvements brought about by strict laws and cleanup initiatives, the river still faces contamination problems during periods of severe rainfall when overflow systems may dump untreated water.

Another issue has been the quality of the air, particularly in the summer months when Richmond occasionally experiences "Code Orange" smog advisories. Ozone generation is caused by elements like vehicle emissions, industrial processes, and even naturally occurring substances like pollen. Vulnerable groups including children, the elderly, and people with respiratory disorders may suffer negative health impacts as a result of exposure to ozone.

Urban sprawl and land use have presented further difficulties. There has been a considerable loss of green space as Richmond and its suburbs have grown, raising worries about habitat destruction, rising temperatures from the 'urban heat island' effect, and aggravated stormwater runoff issues.

Another environmental problem the city faces is waste management. Landfills that are nearly at capacity and the difficulties of recycling, particularly in light of shifting worldwide markets and standards, have compelled Richmond to look for creative ways to reduce waste and to support neighborhood-wide recycling programs.

Richmond is vulnerable to the effects of climate change because of its location. Flooding may result from a rise in the frequency of extreme weather events like hurricanes and powerful storms, especially in low-lying places. The necessity for efficient urban design and infrastructure improvements to reduce possible harm is highlighted by this vulnerability.

There is also a story of perseverance and action hidden within these difficulties. Community organizations, grassroots movements, and environmental nonprofits have been in the forefront of bringing about change and raising awareness. For instance, the James River Association has been crucial in promoting the river's health and has had a great deal of success in doing so.

The municipal government has also demonstrated a dedication to environmental sustainability. Richmond is on a path of continuous environmental improvement, from measures supporting renewable energy and energy efficiency to green infrastructure projects that aim to lessen stormwater runoff and improve water quality.

Despite the huge environmental issues Richmond is facing, citizens, decision-makers, and activists are working together with a common goal to bring hope. The long history of the city and the steady flow of the James River serve as reminders of the need to save and conserve the environment for upcoming generations. The harmony between development and preservation continues to be a key component of Richmond's story as it looks to the future.

Chapter 39: Technological Advancements from Richmond

The important roles Richmond played during colonial times, the Revolutionary War, and the Civil War are frequently cited in the city's historical narrative. A lesser-known tale about Richmond's quiet but vital contributions to technological developments, though, can be found hidden beneath the historical backdrop. The city has made its mark on both the national and international levels over the years as a center of technological expertise and innovation.

Richmond made a significant advancement in transportation throughout the 19th century with the establishment of the Richmond Locomotive Works. This business was fundamental to the development of steam locomotives, which were a vital component of America's rail transportation network. Richmond Locomotive Works had already built thousands of steam engines by the time it amalgamated with other businesses to establish the American Locomotive Company in the early 20th century, helping the fast growth of railroads across the country.

With the establishment of the first profitable electric streetcar system in history, Richmond continued to lead the world in transportation technology well into the 20th century. This invention from the late 1800s, known as the Richmond Union Passenger Railway, not only revolutionized urban transportation in Richmond but also served as a model for other cities all over the world to adopt and improve the electric streetcar design.

The Medical College of Virginia (now a part of Virginia Commonwealth University) has been at the forefront of several key advancements in the fields of medicine and health. The school has constantly advanced medical knowledge, from groundbreaking work in organ transplantation to developments in pharmacology.

In numerous industries, Richmond has embraced technology in the digital age. The Richmond-based Universal Corporation, a major supplier of leaf tobacco, used cutting-edge agronomic techniques and organic farming methods. This improved tobacco quality while also ensuring more ecologically friendly and sustainable agricultural techniques.

The financial industry in Richmond wasn't left behind either. With information-based techniques, Capital One, which was created in the city, transformed credit card marketing in the 1990s. They may personalize offers to particular customers using cutting-edge data analytics, transforming the lending market.

Incubators and tech companies have increased in the city in the twenty-first century. The Richmond Technology Council and Activation Capital have been instrumental in creating an atmosphere that is supportive of tech entrepreneurs. Companies like Health Warrior and CarLotz, both of which have used technology to disrupt established industry sectors, are prime examples of this push for digital innovation.

Dominion Energy, a company with headquarters in Richmond, has constantly made investments in the development of cleaner, more sustainable energy technology, from nuclear to renewable energy sources.

Although Richmond may not be mentioned as often in discussions about innovation centres like Silicon Valley or Boston, its consistent and diversified contributions to technical progress are clear. Richmond's contribution to innovation spans a wide range of industries, including transportation, finance, health, and energy. The city's embrace of technology is expected to continue as it looks to the future, further solidifying its position as an essential contributor to the advancement of technology around the world.

Chapter 40: The Future Outlook for Richmond

Richmond is on the cusp of a number of transformative prospects as it advances towards the latter half of the twenty-first century. Despite having a rich past, Richmond is a city in transition that is prepared to change and grow in response to current issues and wider-ranging trends.

Urban renewal and growth are important priorities for Richmond. There is a need to create sustainable, habitable areas due to the city's expanding population and the influx of young professionals. Older buildings will probably be converted into contemporary offices, apartments, and commercial spaces in a technique called adaptive reuse that has already gained traction, keeping the city's historic beauty.

The economic environment in Richmond is anticipated to diversify even further. Even if the main economic drivers continue to be the legal, financial, and government sectors, there is a clear shift in favor of the technology industry. As more businesses choose Richmond as their home base, the city is poised to develop into a thriving center for digital innovation, supported by encouraging laws and organizations like the Richmond Technology Council.

Many of Richmond's future policies will be influenced by environmental sustainability. The James River continues to be essential to the character of the city. There will be a greater emphasis on improving the river's water quality, preserving its biodiversity, and creating greenways along its banks. These initiatives will not only improve ecological health but also give locals access to more recreational space and ecotourism opportunities.

In the fields of education and research, Richmond is poised to achieve tremendous advancements. In disciplines like health, the arts, and engineering, institutions like Virginia Commonwealth University will keep pushing the envelope. The interaction between academia and business will probably spur innovation and produce real goods and services for international markets.

As the city struggles with the combined issues of urban congestion and the demand for sustainable solutions, transportation will undergo a transformation. Richmond's urban fabric may soon include improved public transportation options, the encouragement of bicycle and pedestrian lanes, and possibly even the incorporation of autonomous vehicles.

The importance of cultural diversity and inclusivity will increase. As the world becomes more globalized, Richmond is going to house a melting pot of cultures and races. Everything from culinary options to festivals, the arts, and even policy-making will be influenced by this variety.

The effects of climate change will be difficult, especially considering Richmond's susceptibility to severe weather. But with a forward-thinking strategy, the city is likely to make investments in planning and infrastructure that reduce hazards and guarantee the security and wellbeing of its citizens.

In essence, innovation, sustainability, diversity, and resilience are the threads that Richmond's future is made of. Despite the challenges that lie ahead, the city is well-positioned to not just face the future but to shape it in a way that honors its illustrious past and lively present because of its deeply ingrained spirit and capacity for adaptation. Richmond aspires to be a city that combines the knowledge of its past with the hope of the future as the pages of this future are written.

Chapter 41: Must-See Locations in Richmond

Location	Address
Virginia State Capitol	1000 Bank St, Richmond, VA 23218
Virginia Museum of Fine Arts (VMFA)	200 N Arthur Ashe Blvd, Richmond, VA 23220
Maymont	1700 Hampton St, Richmond, VA 23220
The Edgar Allan Poe Museum	1914 E Main St, Richmond, VA 23223
Lewis Ginter Botanical Garden	1800 Lakeside Ave, Richmond, VA 23228
Richmond National Battlefield Park	3215 E Broad St, Richmond, VA 23223
Hollywood Cemetery	412 S Cherry St, Richmond, VA 23220
Science Museum of Virginia	2500 W Broad St, Richmond, VA 23220
The American Civil War Museum	500 Tredegar St, Richmond, VA 23219
Agecroft Hall & Gardens	4305 Sulgrave Rd, Richmond, VA 23221
Belle Isle	Tredegar St, Richmond, VA 23219

Don't miss out!

Visit the website below and you can sign up to receive emails whenever Henry Church publishes a new book. There's no charge and no obligation.

https://books2read.com/r/B-A-GDIAB-TCTNC

BOOKS 2 READ

Connecting independent readers to independent writers.

Also by Henry Church

American Cities History Guidebook Series
Charlottesville, Virginia: Historical Guide for Travelers
Williamsburg, Virginia: Historical Guide for Travelers
Richmond, Virginia: Historical Guide for Travelers
Norfolk & Virginia Beach: Historical Guide for Travelers
Winchester, Virginia: Historical Guide for Travelers
Baltimore, Maryland: Historical Guide for Travelers
Dover, Delaware: Historical Guide for Travelers
Arlington, Virginia: Historical Guide for Travelers

About the Publisher

Fiel LLC is dedicated to providing high-quality content at affordable prices, utilizing state-of-the-art processes and advanced content generation systems to ensure a superior reading experience. All books published by Fiel LLC are for entertainment purposes only. Fiel LLC authors use pen names and are not experts in any field, so no content should be taken as financial, medical, legal, or professional advice. All information provided is subject to change, and readers are encouraged to verify the latest details through their own research.

www.ingramcontent.com/pod-product-compliance
Lightning Source LLC
Chambersburg PA
CBHW061329120726
48001CB00002B/758